SEA OF TRANQUILITY

APOLLO 11 LANDING SITE

MAN WALKS ON
THE MOON

MAN WALKS ON THE MOON

ODYSSEYS

VALERIE BODDEN

CREATIVE EDUCATION•CREATIVE PAPERBACKS

Published by Creative Education and Creative Paperbacks
P.O. Box 227, Mankato, Minnesota 56002
Creative Education and Creative Paperbacks
are imprints of The Creative Company
www.thecreativecompany.us

Design and production by Blue Design
Art direction by Rita Marshall
Printed in the United States of America

Photographs by British Library Collection (Emile Antoine
Bayard), Corbis (Bettmann, David J. & Janice L. Frent
Collection, ESA/NASA/Handout/epa, NASA/JPL/CNP), Getty
Images (AFP, Neil A. Armstrong/NASA/Time & Life Pictures,
Hulton Archive, Keystone, NASA-Apollo/digital version by
Science Faction, NASA/Newsmakers, NASA/Space Frontiers,
NASA/Time & Life Pictures, Popperfoto, Arnold Sachs/
Keystone/CNP, Space Frontiers, Time & Life Pictures), NASA
(Apollo 11, Earth Sciences Web Team, Björn Jónsson/NASA/
JPL, Lockheed Martin, NASA, Kipp Teague), Wikimedia
Creative Commons (NASA)

Library of Congress Cataloging-in-Publication Data
Bodden, Valerie.
Man walks on the moon / Valerie Bodden.
p. cm. — (Odysseys in history)
Summary: A look at the causes and global effects of the
1969 moon landing, which led to further space exploration
and eventually encouraged international cooperation rather
than competition.
Includes bibliographical references and index.
ISBN 978-1-60818-528-3 (hardcover)
ISBN 978-1-62832-129-6 (pbk)
1. Project Apollo (U.S.)—Juvenile literature. 2. Apollo 11
(Spacecraft)—Juvenile literature. 3. Space flight to the moon—
Juvenile literature. I. Title.

TL789.8.U6A52194 2015
629.45′4—dc23   2014041766

CCSS: RI.8.1, 2, 3, 4; RI.9-10.1, 2, 3, 4; RI.11-12.1, 2, 3, 4; RH.6-8.1, 4,
5, 7; RH.9-10.1, 3, 4

First Edition HC 9 8 7 6 5 4 3 2 1
First Edition PBK 9 8 7 6 5 4 3 2 1

Cover: Buzz Aldrin walking on the moon
Page 2: A boot print from the Apollo 11 mission
Pages 4–5: Buzz Aldrin descending from the lunar module

CONTENTS

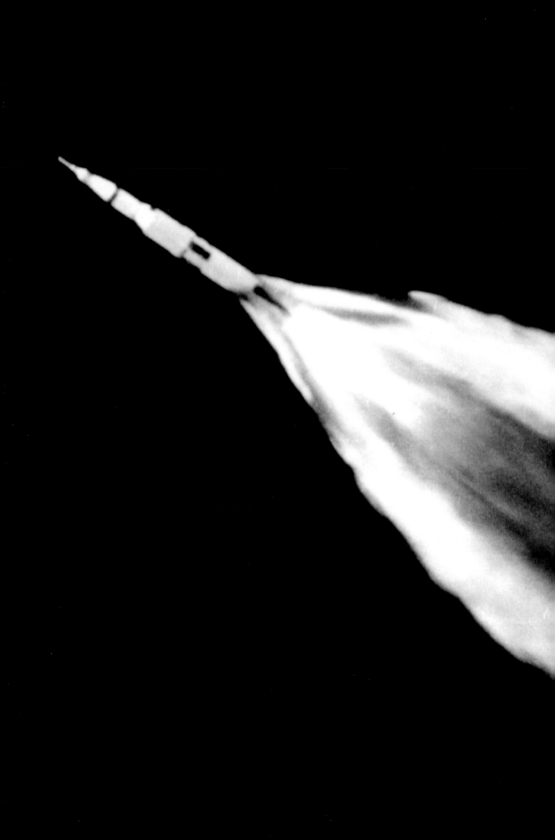

Introduction

It was 10:56 P.M. Eastern time on Sunday, July 20, 1969, and people around the world were glued to their televisions. The picture on their screens was black-and-white and fuzzy, but that didn't matter. They were watching history in the making. As millions on Earth held their breath, a lone spacesuit-clad figure descended a ladder and planted his left boot firmly on the surface of the moon. As he did so,

OPPOSITE: On July 16, 1969, the Saturn V rocket carrying three American astronauts launched into space on the historic Apollo 11 lunar mission.

American astronaut Neil Armstrong said the words that would forever be linked to the first moon landing: "That's one small step for [a] man, one giant leap for mankind."

Armstrong's historic walk on the moon followed a decade of intense dedication to the goal of reaching the lunar surface. Yet, even as most of the world rejoiced at the accomplishment, some argued that the money spent on a moon mission could better be spent closer to home. Within 4 years, astronauts were no longer making the 240,000-mile (386,000 km) journey to the moon, and future missions on the space shuttle were limited to within 400 miles (640 km) of Earth. Today, though, the dream of space exploration has been revived, and America's space program has once again set its sights on the moon—and beyond.

July 20, 1969

The Race for Space

Man's first steps on a body in space came at a time when life on Earth was in turmoil. Wars, protests, and civil unrest shook much of the world, and an intense rivalry known as the Cold War simmered between the democratic United States and the communist Soviet Union. Tensions mounted as each superpower amassed huge stores of nuclear weapons and sought to spread its own system of government around the globe.

In the U.S., the Cold War was just one source of tension, as the decade of the 1960s brought with it domestic troubles as well. During the early years of the decade, America—and especially the South—was still split largely along racial lines, with blacks facing discrimination in housing, schooling, and job opportunities. Although many at first turned to the peaceful civil rights movement led by Martin Luther King Jr. in an attempt to bring about change, some soon concluded that peaceful methods were not doing enough. Leaders such as Malcolm X began to call for more drastic measures. By the middle of the decade, race riots were rocking cities from Los Angeles to Detroit, as largely black crowds burned and looted homes and businesses in their own neighborhoods. After King was assassinated in 1968, rioting became even more widespread, reaching 29 states and leading to 46 deaths and 2,600 injuries.

- -

"Without denying the value of scientific endeavor, there is a striking absurdity in committing billions to reach the moon where no people live, while only a fraction of that amount is appropriated to service the densely populated slums."

Martin Luther King Jr., civil rights activist, 1967

- -

The civil rights movement was not the only source of protest in America during the '60s. Demonstrators across the country also opposed America's involvement in the Vietnam War. Some protests were nonviolent, such as those led by "hippies," people who rejected authority and often lived in communes, where many experimented with drugs. Hippies, many of whom were youths, handed out flowers to police officers and other authority figures, encouraging them to "make love, not war." Other protests, often led by college students, involved bloody clashes with police.

eanwhile, only 90 miles (145 km) south of the U.S., in communist Cuba, citizens living under Prime Minister Fidel Castro's regime were provided with access to schools, healthcare, and public transportation but faced shortages of necessities such as food, clothing, and gasoline. Beginning in 1968, Castro

Orbiting Earth

Although space might seem to be far from Earth, the edge of outer space is only 62 miles (100 km) above the planet's surface. At this altitude, Earth's atmosphere—the protective shield of air that surrounds the planet—becomes very thin. Just above this, at altitudes up to 1,240 miles (2,000 km), objects such as the International Space Station circle the globe in Low Earth Orbit. At heights of 1,240 to 22,236 miles (2,000–35,785 km), navigation satellites move in Medium Earth Orbit, and at an altitude of 22,236 miles (35,785 km), communications satellites travel in geosynchronous orbits (meaning that they circle Earth once each day).

attempted to bring more money into the island nation by increasing sugar production. Many Cubans were forced to take time off from their regular work to labor in the country's sugar fields, unpaid.

Across the Atlantic Ocean, citizens in Cuba's communist ally, the Soviet Union, fared much the same. Although communism was supposed to ensure that all citizens were treated equally, most people found themselves struggling to eke out a living—facing food shortages and being forced to work in corrupt government-run businesses—even as government leaders lived in luxury. The people had no way to express their displeasure with their circumstances, either; those who spoke out against the government often found themselves imprisoned and sometimes even exiled.

Despite the relative poverty of its citizens, the Soviet Union remained a strong country, with a large army. It used its power to ensure that the neighboring countries of Eastern Europe—which had been brought under Soviet influence following the end of World War II in 1945—remained communist. During the early 1960s, the Soviets backed the construction of the Berlin Wall by communist East Germany in order to prevent citizens from escaping to democratic West Germany. Then, in 1968, Soviet troops invaded Czechoslovakia, crushing a peaceful reform movement

that had introduced greater freedom of speech and more contact with democratic nations.

Meanwhile, in eastern Asia, communism was also gaining power. China, which had been taken over by communist rule in 1949, embarked on a "Cultural Revolution" in 1966. During the Revolution, all signs of traditional Chinese culture were destroyed in an attempt to keep Chinese citizens loyal to communism. And, to the south of China, in the jungles of Vietnam, a bloody civil war raged, as communist North Vietnam attempted to take over the democratic South. The Soviet Union supported North Vietnam, while the South was aided by American troops, as the U.S. feared that if South Vietnam fell to communism, all of Southeast Asia would soon follow.

Even as the U.S. and the Soviet Union confronted one another in the Vietnamese jungle, they were also involved in an intense struggle in an even more exotic locale: space. In October 1957, the Soviet Union had ignited the space race with its launch of *Sputnik 1*, the world's first artificial satellite. The U.S. reeled at the news, knowing that a missile capable of launching a satellite into space was also capable of sending a nuclear warhead across the world. Only a month later, the Soviets launched *Sputnik 2*, which carried a dog named Laika, making her the first living creature in space.

"I think one of the things we had was a common goal; and we all realized that we were into something that was one of the few things in history that was going to stand out over the years. We're going to go to the moon! We're putting a man on the moon! And that so captured our imagination, and our emotion, that we didn't want to go home at night. We just wanted to keep going, and we couldn't wait to get up and get back at work in the morning—because we're going to the moon!"

Charlie Mars, chief lunar module project engineer at Kennedy Space Center during Project Apollo, February 2004

The U.S. rushed to catch up with Soviet space technology, launching its own small satellite, *Explorer 1*, in 1958 and forming the National Aeronautics and Space Administration (NASA) that same year. Yet the Soviets continued to outpace the Americans in space, sending the unmanned *Luna* spacecraft to the moon in 1959 and boosting the first human, cosmonaut Yuri Gagarin, into Earth orbit in April 1961. The U.S. was a month behind, as American Alan Shepard became the second man in space in May, on a flight that lasted only 15 minutes. It would be another nine months before John Glenn became the first American to orbit the planet. After a careful review of America's space program and its potential for surpassing that of the Soviets, president John F. Kennedy made a dramatic announcement on May 25, 1961: "I believe that this nation should commit itself to achieving

Aerospace Employees

At the height of the Apollo program in the mid-1960s, more than 400,000 people were involved in making manned moon missions possible. About 36,000 of them were employed by NASA, while others worked for aerospace contractors and other companies hired by the space agency. Today, NASA employs less than half that number, with a full-time workforce of about 18,000. Another 60,000 people work with the agency under contracts or grants. Headquartered in Washington, D.C., NASA today has facilities across the U.S., including Ames Research Center in California, Johnson Space Center in Texas, Kennedy Space Center in Florida, and Marshall Space Flight Center in Alabama.

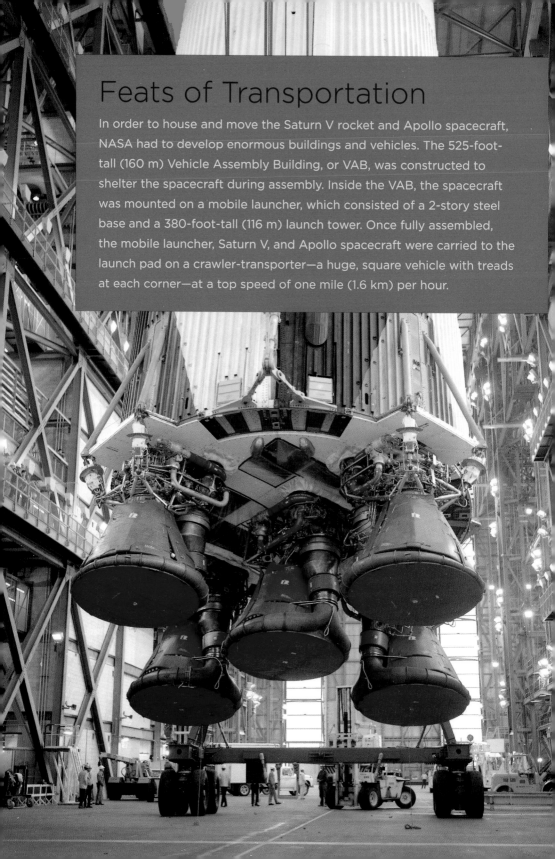

Feats of Transportation

In order to house and move the Saturn V rocket and Apollo spacecraft, NASA had to develop enormous buildings and vehicles. The 525-foot-tall (160 m) Vehicle Assembly Building, or VAB, was constructed to shelter the spacecraft during assembly. Inside the VAB, the spacecraft was mounted on a mobile launcher, which consisted of a 2-story steel base and a 380-foot-tall (116 m) launch tower. Once fully assembled, the mobile launcher, Saturn V, and Apollo spacecraft were carried to the launch pad on a crawler-transporter—a huge, square vehicle with treads at each corner—at a top speed of one mile (1.6 km) per hour.

the goal, before this decade is out, of landing a man on the moon and returning him safely to the earth."

NASA astronauts and engineers immediately set out to accomplish this goal. From 1961 to 1966, a series of manned flights aboard the Mercury and Gemini spacecraft proved that human beings could survive long periods of space travel and helped the first astronauts develop the skills they would need on the voyage to the moon. At the same time, unmanned probes were sent to the moon to photograph and examine the lunar surface in search of potential landing sites.

Finally, NASA was ready to begin Project Apollo, the program that would bring the dramatic vision announced by Kennedy (who had been assassinated in 1963) to fruition. Unfortunately, the first mission of that program went terribly wrong when a fire broke out in the

Apollo 1 craft during a training exercise in 1967, killing the three astronauts inside. As a result, the spacecraft underwent more than 1,000 design changes and was sent on 3 unmanned flights (Apollos 4, 5, and 6) before again being loaded with a live crew. In October 1968, Apollo 7 became the first manned Apollo mission when it circled Earth for 11 days. Only two months later, the crew of Apollo 8 lifted off, headed for the moon. On Christmas Eve, they reached their target, becoming the first humans to ever see the far side of the moon (the same side of the moon always faces Earth) as they orbited 69 miles (111 km) above its surface. They sent back television feed of its hills and craters, as they recited the opening verses of the biblical book of Genesis in the background.

n March 1969, Apollo 9 rocketed into Earth orbit to test the lunar module, the part of the spacecraft that would actually land on the moon. Two months later, Apollo 10 became the second manned mission to reach the moon. Its lunar module descended to within 50,000 feet (15,240 m) of the lunar surface, flying at nearly the same altitude that commercial flights travel over Earth. With that crew's safe return home, the dress rehearsals for the moon landing were complete. All that remained was to put a man on the moon.

One Small Step

Nearly a million people crowded
the beaches and open grounds
of Florida near Cape Canaveral
on the morning of July 16, 1969.
All of them trained their eyes
toward Launch Complex 39 at
the Kennedy Space Center, where
a towering Saturn V rocket was
being prepared to launch the
Apollo 11 mission to the moon.
With just over two hours remaining
until they would fly into history,

OPPOSITE: Apollo 11's Saturn V produced about 7.6 million
pounds (3.4 million kg) of thrust, or upward force, when it
launched from the Kennedy Space Center.

Apollo 11's crew boarded the launch tower elevator. It carried them 36 stories to the spacecraft's gumdrop-shaped command module, named *Columbia*, in which they would journey to the moon. The tiny craft, which was less than 13 feet (4 m) across at its base and stood only 11.5 feet (3.5 m) tall, barely had enough room to comfortably seat the 3 crew members—Mission Commander Neil Armstrong, Edwin "Buzz" Aldrin, and Michael Collins. Yet this small space would have to serve as the astronauts' cockpit, cargo hold, and sleeping quarters during their three-day journey to the moon. Fortunately, all but a few minutes of that journey would take place under zero-gravity conditions, and in the weightlessness of space, the astronauts would be able to move about in every available area of the craft—including in midair.

"[The decision to go to the moon] was far from a romantic decision. It was a very cold-blooded calculation that the honor, power, and prestige of the United States required that we be first in space. Kennedy calculated that space was a symbol of national power, national vitality in the 20th century, and that the United States, if that was the symbolic quotient of national power, had to be first there."

Dr. John Logsdon, assistant professor of politics at the Catholic University of America, July 20, 1969

First, though, the astronauts had to get into space. At 9:32 A.M., the powerful first stage of the Saturn V rocket ignited, its five gigantic F-1 engines roaring to life. Slowly, the entire 363-foot-tall (110 m) assembly—the Saturn V topped by the Apollo spacecraft—began to lift off the ground, rising on a column of fire. Soon, the rocket began to pick up speed, soaring to a height of 42 miles (68 km) above Earth's surface in just two and a half minutes.

- -

"When the moment came which everybody had been waiting for, it seemed to stun them into a kind of frozen disbelief. They couldn't quite believe that man was finally on his way to worlds outside the one where he began. And as it rose higher and higher it began finally to move the eyes upward…. It was the poetry of hope, if you will, unspoken but seen in the kind of concentrated gestures that people had as they reached up and up with the rocket."

Heywood Hale Broun, CBS news commentator, on the launch of Apollo 11, July 16, 1969

- -

Then, with its fuel spent, the first stage of the Saturn V was jettisoned into the Atlantic Ocean. The rocket's second stage fired, powering the spacecraft to a speed

Different Demeanors

Although Neil Armstrong, Michael Collins, and Buzz Aldrin (pictured above, left to right) were all born in 1930 and had all been pilots for the U.S. military before joining NASA, they had very different personalities. Armstrong was quiet and focused, Aldrin was analytical and scholarly, and Collins was outgoing and easy to talk to. Soon after their historic flight, all three astronauts retired from NASA and went their own ways. Armstrong taught aerospace engineering and served as chairman of Computing Technologies for Aviation, Aldrin served as president of a private company that works to revitalize the space program, and Collins directed the National Air & Space Museum in Washington, D.C.

of 15,000 miles (24,000 km) per hour and bringing it to an altitude of 117 miles (188 km) only 9 minutes after the rocket had left the ground. The second stage then also broke off and fell toward the Atlantic, as the rocket's third stage sent the craft on an orbit around Earth. While in orbit, the astronauts checked their spacecraft to make sure that all systems had withstood the force of liftoff.

When Armstrong and his crew were satisfied that their craft was in good shape—and once they had gotten the go-ahead from mission control in Houston, Texas—the third stage of the rocket accelerated Apollo 11 to a speed of 24,000 miles (38,600 km) per hour, breaking it out of Earth orbit.

"Looking at Earth from space was so much like looking at the big globe in my office that I found myself searching for the lines that divided Georgia from Florida, California from Nevada, and Mozambique from Malawi. There were no dividing lines, however. Seen from the perspective of space, political, racial, linguistic, and religious divisions all disappear. Looking at Earth from high up, I saw only one globe—a planet that is itself a fragile spaceship in the black void of space."

Bill Nelson, U.S. senator who flew on the space shuttle *Columbia*, 1988

Then the engine was discarded, and the spacecraft coasted toward the moon. For three days, the astronauts

OPPOSITE After *Eagle* separated from *Columbia*, Collins took photographs of the descending lunar module, the lunar surface, and the distant but brightly colored Earth.

traveled through the void of space, living in *Columbia* and relying on the attached service module to provide them with vital oxygen and water.

Finally, on July 19, Apollo 11 approached the moon and entered lunar orbit. The next afternoon, Armstrong and Aldrin climbed into the craft's spider-shaped lunar module, named *Eagle*. Collins, still aboard *Columbia*, pressed a switch that separated the two parts of the spacecraft, radioing "See you later" to his crewmates. Standing in the cockpit of the *Eagle* (the seats had been removed to save weight), Armstrong and Aldrin were even more crowded than they had been in the *Columbia*. But the two men didn't have time to think about that now; they had to focus on landing their craft safely on the moon.

Armstrong and Aldrin stared intently out the *Eagle*'s triangular windows at the lunar landscape, which was marked by sharp shadows in the bright sunlight of the lunar morning (the lunar day and night each last 14 Earth days). Realizing that the craft's computer was about to land them on a rough, boulder-strewn site that could destroy the lander, Armstrong quickly turned off the autopilot and took manual control of the *Eagle*. As he searched for a better landing site, *Eagle*'s computer began to issue overload alarms, but after a few tense seconds, Houston confirmed that these alarms were not critical to the craft's operation. The *Eagle* was still "go" for landing—but that landing had to come soon, as the craft's landing-engine fuel tank was almost completely empty. From Houston, Armstrong and Aldrin heard a firm, calm voice say, "60 seconds." Then, "30 seconds." Still, Armstrong hadn't found the perfect landing spot. Finally, with only 17 seconds of fuel to spare, Armstrong

Conspiracy Theorists

According to a 1999 survey, 6 percent of Americans think the Apollo moon landings were faked. Some believe that the footage of Neil Armstrong stepping onto the moon was filmed in a Hollywood movie studio. Among their "proof" that astronauts never reached the moon are the facts that no stars are visible in photos taken from the lunar surface and that the flag the astronauts planted appears to ripple, even though there is no wind on the moon. In response, NASA says that the stars are too faint to see in photos and that the flag "ripples" because it is held out by a wire support.

set the *Eagle* down on the southern edge of a vast lunar plain called the Sea of Tranquility. Moments later, he spoke into his radio: "Houston, Tranquility Base here. The *Eagle* has landed." Man was finally on the moon.

Although what many had considered to be the hardest part of the mission was done, Armstrong and Aldrin couldn't relax yet. They had to check their craft to be sure it was ready for an emergency return flight (using the lunar module's liftoff engine), should that be necessary. When that task was completed, the astronauts were supposed to rest, but with their adrenaline pumping as they looked out at the strange new world they had traveled so far to reach, the astronauts requested—and were granted—permission to begin their moonwalk early.

Before they could even open the hatch of the *Eagle*, though, the two men had to make sure that they were properly sealed into their Extravehicular Mobility Units (EMUs), or spacesuits. Consisting of a water-cooled undergarment, a 17-layer pressure suit, a bubble-shaped helmet, and a backpack containing life-sustaining oxygen, the EMUs offered the astronauts protection from the hazards of the lunar surface. Without the suits, the moon's lack of air, radiation from the sun, micrometeoroids (tiny, incredibly fast-moving pieces of rock), or extreme temperatures (ranging from 243 °F, or 117 °C, at lunar noon to -279 °F,

or -173 °C, during the lunar night) would have killed the astronauts almost instantaneously.

With their spacesuits on, Armstrong and Aldrin finally opened the hatch of the *Eagle*, and Armstrong carefully backed out of the cockpit, making his televised descent to the lunar surface. The sky above him was pitch-black, interrupted only by the gleaming blue Earth, which floated like a tiny ball far above. At his feet, moon dust stretched for miles in every direction, littered with thousands of rocks and indented by numerous craters. As he gazed at his surroundings, Armstrong reported back to Earth: "It has a stark beauty all its own. It's like much of the high desert of the United States. It's different, but it's very pretty out here."

"You get a feeling that people think of these men [astronauts] as not just superior men but different creatures. They are like people who have gone into the other world and have returned, and you sense they bear secrets that we will never entirely know, that they will never entirely be able to explain."

Eric Sevareid, CBS news national correspondent, July 16, 1969

About 20 minutes later, Aldrin joined Armstrong on the surface, and the 2 astronauts got to work, spending the next two and a half hours snapping photographs, collecting rocks, and setting up experiments to measure

Science-Fiction Prophecies

Long before travel to the moon became a reality, visionary authors wrote about voyages to the lunar surface. A century before the launch of Apollo 11, French author Jules Verne wrote *From the Earth to the Moon* and *Round the Moon*, about three men who use a cannon to launch themselves around the moon. Verne's novels inspired rocket scientists and engineers to seek ways to turn science fiction into reality. When they finally did so, they discovered that some aspects of his novels, including the Florida launch site, the three-man crew, and the splashdown in the Pacific Ocean, had been prophetic.

moonquakes, calculate the exact Earth-to-moon distance, and collect solar wind (particles of the sun that flow into space). The two men soon figured out that on the moon, where the force of gravity is only one-sixth as strong as on Earth, hopping or bounding was easier and more efficient than walking. All too soon, though, it was time to return to the lunar module to rest and prepare for the trip home.

The next afternoon, Armstrong and Aldrin fired the *Eagle*'s liftoff engine, and the craft rose from the landing stage of the lunar module, which served as their launch pad into lunar orbit. As the two moon explorers lifted off from the lunar surface, they left behind an American flag, some of their equipment, and a tiny disc with messages from world leaders inscribed on it. On one of the legs of the landing stage was a plaque reading, "Here men from the planet Earth first set foot upon the moon. July 1969 A.D. We came in peace for all mankind."

- -

"I remember this fleeting thought from the surface of the moon: the two of us, Neil and I, are farther away than two humans have ever been before, not just in distance but in what we have to do to get back, and yet there are more people paying attention to what we are doing now than have ever paid attention to other people before."

Buzz Aldrin, Apollo 11 astronaut, 2007

- -

Exploring the Universe

Just over seven minutes after leaving the surface of the moon, Armstrong and Aldrin entered lunar orbit. About three and a half hours later, they rendezvoused with the *Columbia*, where Collins had spent the past 24 hours orbiting the moon. Collins lined up his craft's docking hatch with the *Eagle*'s, and the two spacecraft came slowly together. After they docked, Armstrong and Aldrin moved back

OPPOSITE: Upon setting foot on the moon's surface, Buzz Aldrin famously described the stark, crater-filled landscape as "magnificent desolation."

into the *Columbia*, and the *Eagle* was jettisoned. Another three-day journey brought the Apollo 11 astronauts back to Earth on July 24, 1969. Of the entire 6-million-pound (2.7 million kg) Saturn V and Apollo assemblage that had ascended from the launch pad 8 days before, only the 12,000-pound (5,450 kg) command module returned. (The service module was also released in space.) After a fiery reentry into Earth's atmosphere, during which temperatures on the outside of the craft reached 5,000 °F (2,760 °C), the *Columbia* splashed down in the Pacific Ocean, where the three astronauts were taken aboard the aircraft carrier USS *Hornet*.

Although the world was eager to greet the returning heroes, Armstrong, Aldrin, and Collins were quickly carried away to a three-week quarantine to ensure that they hadn't brought back any "moon germs." (They hadn't.) Congratulatory messages poured into the U.S. from around the world, as more than 100 foreign leaders called to express their admiration for the American achievement. Even the Soviets were impressed by the Apollo 11 mission, as the state-run *Pravda* newspaper in Moscow announced, "We rejoice at the success of the American astronauts."

What the Soviet newspaper didn't say was that Project Apollo had brought about a stunning American victory in the space race. Instead, the Soviets pretended that they had never been involved in a race to the moon,

The three Apollo 11 astronauts were quickly locked into a Mobile Quarantine Facility on the deck of the *Hornet*, where they were soon joking with president Richard Nixon.

It wasn't until 1989 that the communist nation admitted that it had been racing to reach the moon but hadn't succeeded.

even as work on their moon program secretly continued until 1974. It wasn't until 1989 that the communist nation admitted that it had been racing to reach the moon but hadn't succeeded.

Now that it had won the space race, the U.S. was ready to send more men to the moon to explore its surface more thoroughly. More Apollo spacecraft were readied, as even the lone Apollo command module that returned to Earth couldn't be reused after enduring the scorching heat of reentry. Only months after the return of Apollo 11, Apollo 12 was launched, completing another successful moon mission in November 1969.

Although the next mission, Apollo 13, never made
it to the moon because of a midair explosion that almost
stranded its three crew members in space, four more moon
missions—Apollos 14 through 17—met with success.
Landing on different parts of the moon, the astronauts on
these missions explored huge, rolling lunar mountains and
looked into deep canyons. With a better understanding of

the moon and improved gear, the astronauts spent longer and longer periods on the lunar surface—up to three days. This allowed them to take part in more moonwalks and greatly increased the number of experiments they could set up. Astronauts on Apollo missions 15, 16, and 17 were also able to make use of the new lunar roving vehicle, a kind of "moon buggy," which allowed them to cover more area on each moonwalk.

n total, the 12 astronauts who landed on the moon brought back more than 840 pounds (380 kg) of rock and dust samples, from which scientists discovered

Unmanned Missions

Even while pursuing manned space flight, NASA has sent a
number of unmanned missions into space. Beginning in the 1960s,
Mariner probes were sent past Mercury, Venus, and Mars. In 1976,
two Viking spacecraft landed on Mars, mapping its surface. Since
that time, a number of additional unmanned craft have landed on
Mars, and probes have flown past every planet in the solar system.
In 2013, scientists confirmed that *Voyager 1* had entered interstellar
space, making it the most distant unmanned spacecraft ever
to operate. As of 2015, the craft continued to return surprising
information to Earth.

Although Apollo missions 18, 19, and 20 had been planned, they were canceled, and NASA turned its attention to a new priority: a space shuttle.

that many of the minerals that are found on Earth are also found on the moon, but in different proportions. They also learned that most of the craters on the lunar surface were formed by collisions with space debris, not volcanoes, as had been hypothesized. In addition to what they brought back to Earth, the Apollo missions were also important for what they left behind: experiments and instruments that could relay information such as seismic readings and heat flow measurements from the lunar surface back to Earth.

Despite the success of the $25-billion Apollo program, by the early 1970s, interest in manned moon missions had waned. With mounting concerns about problems on Earth—such as the continuing Vietnam War, riots, and pollution—the government cut NASA's budget. Although Apollo missions 18, 19, and 20 had been planned, they were canceled, and NASA turned its attention to a new priority: a space shuttle. Unlike the Apollo spacecraft, the space shuttle would be reusable, and instead of journeying to the moon, it would orbit Earth at a maximum altitude of 400 miles (640 km). Although the space shuttle was originally scheduled to be built by 1978, a number of delays pushed its completion back to 1981. When it was finished, the shuttle could hold a crew of up to

The lunar rover used on the Apollo 17 mission enabled astronauts to drive across 22 miles (35 km) of lunar terrain and collect more than 240 pounds (109 kg) of moon rock.

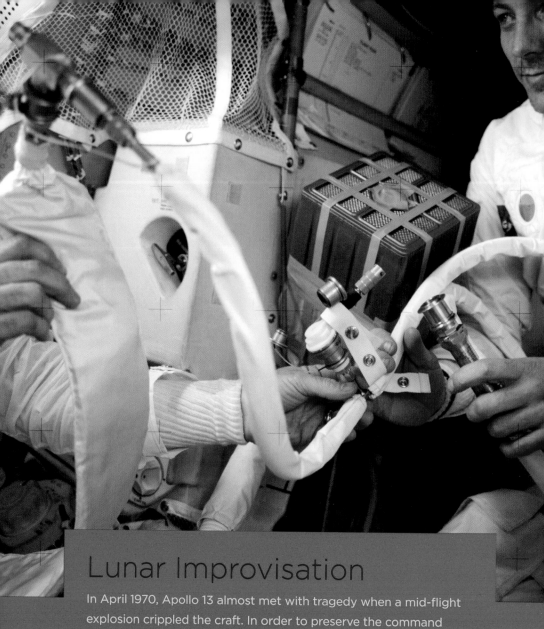

Lunar Improvisation

In April 1970, Apollo 13 almost met with tragedy when a mid-flight explosion crippled the craft. In order to preserve the command module's little remaining power for reentry, the crew had to move into the lunar module, where they faced freezing temperatures and a lack of water. Their biggest problem occurred when they ran out of the round filters needed to remove poisonous carbon dioxide from the air. With only the command module's square-shaped filters available, the crew improvised an adapter from a flight plan cover, a sock, a plastic bag, and duct tape. The fix worked, and after three tense days, the astronauts returned safely to Earth.

seven astronauts and could transport satellites or space observatories into space. It was used for this purpose throughout the early 1980s.

"To an 'Earthling,' one of the moon's most striking features was its stillness. With no atmosphere and no wind, the only movements we could detect on the lunar surface, apart from our own, were the gradually shifting shadows ... There were no other features: no trees, bushes, rivers, streams, flowers, grass, animals, or birds—none of the signs of nature that human beings ... are used to. There was no sound, either, apart from the gentle humming of the equipment in our backpacks. There were no clouds, haze, or mist, and there appeared to be no color."

David Scott, Apollo 15 mission commander, 2004

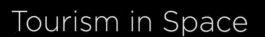

Tourism in Space

Although space travel was once out of reach for anyone but professional astronauts, today Virginia-based Space Adventures offers anyone the opportunity to become a "space tourist"—for a price. For $102,000, tourists can ride into suborbital space (62 miles, or 100 km, above Earth), where they experience up to five minutes of weightlessness. Those willing to spend more—$30 to $40 million—can fly aboard a Russian spacecraft to the International Space Station, an opportunity nine people had taken advantage of as of late 2015. And, for $100 million, a tourist may be able to travel around the moon in the not-too-distant future.

Then, in 1986, disaster struck, as the space shuttle *Challenger* exploded just over a minute after liftoff, killing all seven astronauts on board. For two years, shuttle flights were grounded as NASA investigated the problem. Although flights finally resumed in 1988, NASA greatly scaled back the number of launches it carried out every year by declining to carry commercial or military satellites into orbit; its purpose now was to haul only scientific equipment into space. Shuttle flights continued at a pace of about 6 a year for the next 15 years, until disaster struck again in 2003, with the disintegration of the space shuttle *Columbia* during reentry. Again, all seven crew members were killed, and again, shuttle flights were suspended for two years, resuming in 2005.

The International Space Station includes an acre (0.4 ha) of solar arrays, and NASA hoped to utilize the station until at least 2024.

Circling the planet in Low Earth Orbit ..., the ISS is constructed of several modules that were added one at a time while in space.

Since 2000, the majority of space shuttle flights have been to the International Space Station (ISS), a joint venture begun in 1998 by the space agencies of the U.S., Russia (the Soviet Union had disbanded in 1991), Japan, Europe, and Canada. Circling the planet in Low Earth Orbit (about 240 miles, or 385 km, up), the ISS is constructed of several modules that were added one at a time while in space. Most of the modules hold research stations designed to study such things as the effects of extended weightlessness on humans, the development of new drugs, and the deforestation of Earth. The ISS was completed in 2011 and houses a crew of six. It is about the length and width of a football field.

Even as construction continued on the ISS during the early years of the 21st century, NASA shifted its priorities once again. The space agency retired the shuttle program in 2011 and began work on a new crew vehicle called *Orion* (designed to look much like a larger version of the Apollo spacecraft), which completed its first test flight in December 2014. A manned moon mission was expected to take place after 2020, with the establishment of a permanent lunar base at the moon's south pole by 2024. Eventually, NASA even plans to send manned missions to Mars and beyond, with *Orion*'s help.

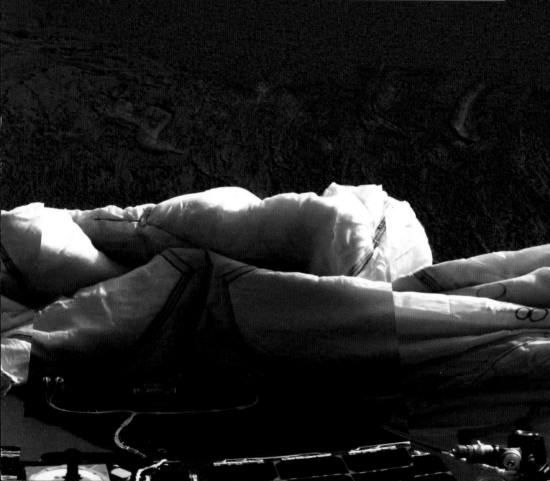

Red Planet Road Trip

Although NASA is planning for an eventual manned mission to Mars, achieving this goal will be difficult. At their closest, Mars and Earth are about 35 million miles (56 million km) apart, which means that a flight to Mars will take 6 months. During this time, astronauts will have to deal with the hazards of radiation and bone deterioration due to extended periods of weightlessness. Once astronauts arrive on the "red planet," they will face a lack of oxygen, subzero temperatures, and frequent dust storms. They will also have to remain on Mars for up to two years before the window for a return journey opens.

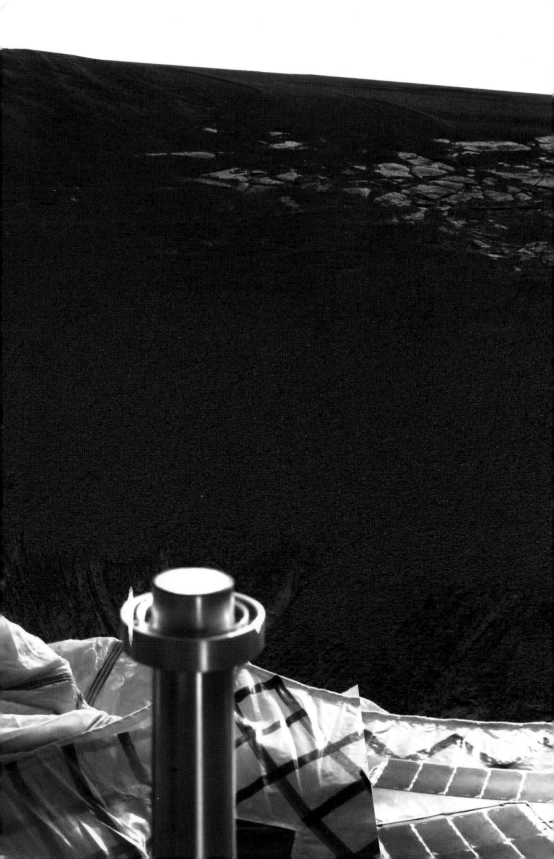

"America is proud of our space program. The risk takers and visionaries of this agency [NASA] have expanded human knowledge, have revolutionized our understanding of the universe, and produced technological advances that have benefited all of humanity. Inspired by all that has come before, and guided by clear objectives, today we set a new course for America's space program.... We will build new ships to carry man forward into the universe, to gain a new foothold on the moon, and to prepare for new journeys to worlds beyond our own."

U.S. president George W. Bush, January 14, 2004

Although the majority of Americans support plans for manned moon and Mars missions, some argue that such missions are a frivolous waste of money that could

be spent solving problems closer to home, such as crime, poverty, pollution, unemployment, and war. Others believe that the money devoted to space exploration would serve humans better if it were earmarked for Earth-bound research in genetics, oceanography, geology, or biology. Even some proponents of space exploration believe that the new direction in space travel is misguided, as they feel that unmanned missions, which cost far less than manned missions, could achieve much more in terms of collecting solid scientific data. Despite these arguments, though, space exploration continues to call out to the human desire for adventure, and, if all goes according to plan, a new generation will soon experience the thrill of watching humans land on the moon.